Praise for *You Are My Joy and Pain*

"Madgett's poems present themselves with an honest approachable ease, and then comes the light, and the wish that you had the wisdom to craft these gems hard pressed under molten heat to make them into the diamonds that result. They are accessible works of art that grant the reader to understand love and pain. The reader will know after reflection that he or she is in the presence of a master."

—Herbert Woodward Martin, author of
The Shape of Regret (Wayne State University Press, 2019)

"Even with the evidence of over a half-century or more of first-rate poetic artistry by Madgett, this collection is a breath-arresting surprise and delight. Poem-by-poem and section-by-section amaze. Each poem in the collection is a master class in technique and in her ability to transpose an idea into a tightly composed example of the craft of poetry."

—Bill Harris, 2011 Kresge Foundation Eminent Artist

"Naomi Long Madgett is a prolific and iconic force in American poetry. The publication of her tenth collection at the age of 97 is possibly an unparalleled event. This work is a blessing that assures that the range, depth, profundity of her voice, and complex subtlety of her poetics will continue to impact, nourish, and advance literary vision."

—Melba Joyce Boyd, poet laureate, Charles H. Wright
Museum of African American History

"Love's blossoming thrills, passionate commitments, and painful demise form the arc of Naomi Long Madgett's *You Are My Joy and Pain* and reflect a lifetime of love. Honesty, wit, and formal dexterity undergird these poems. I especially love how Madgett's steadiness of spirit endures throughout, like 'bread that will sustain.'"

—Terry Blackhawk, author of *One Less River*

"An epic expiration of love and obsession. A masterful achievement by an indomitable spirit."

—Toi Derricotte, author of *I: New and Selected Poems*

YOU ARE MY JOY AND PAIN

Made in Michigan Writers Series

GENERAL EDITORS

Michael Delp, Interlochen Center for the Arts
M. L. Liebler, Wayne State University

A complete listing of the books in this series can be found online at wsupress.wayne.edu

POETRY BY NAOMI LONG MADGETT

Songs to a Phantom Nightingale
One and the Many
Star by Star
Pink Ladies in the Afternoon
Phantom Nightingale: Juvenilia
Exits and Entrances
Octavia and Other Poems
Octavia: Guthrie and Beyond
Remembrances of Spring: Collected Early Poems
Connected Islands: New and Selected Poems

YOU ARE MY JOY AND PAIN

LOVE POEMS
NAOMI LONG MADGETT

WAYNE STATE UNIVERSITY PRESS
DETROIT

ISBN 978-0-8143-4801-7 (paperback)
ISBN 978-0-8143-4802-4 (e-book)

Library of Congress Control Number: 2020938982

All of these poems have appeared in previous collections by this poet. The title of the collection comes from a line in the song "Don't Explain," made popular by Billie Holiday.

Publication of this book was made possible by a generous gift from The Meijer Foundation.

Wayne State University Press
Leonard N. Simons Building
4809 Woodward Avenue
Detroit, Michigan 48201-1309

Visit us online at wsupress.wayne.edu

CONTENTS

A Promise of Sun

Trinity: A Dream Sequence

Stormy Weather

A PROMISE
OF SUN

Heart-Blossom

First love came timidly and full of fear—
love, the late bud that felt its time to grow
was past and shuddered in December's cold.
But then, when warmer turned the ripening year,
up from the seed my heart had dared to sow
burst the full blossom, colorful and bold.

I care not where or how the leaves may fall
or when the petals that I clutch may fade
and hide their perished loveliness in gloom.
I have possessed a love grown clean and tall,
kissed by pure sunlight, strong and unafraid.
I have grown lush and warmer with its bloom.

Good News

The headlines never say good morning anymore.
Every day the forecast reads: *A chance of showers.*
The Tigers keep losing the ball games
and Dick Tracy is reported missing,
his smashed wrist radio recovered
from a burned-out crater of the moon.
The market has plunged again;
clad dimes and quarters have replaced the real ones.

Then you ring the doorbell with a Sunday sunrise
rolled up casually in one pocket
and a handful of silver coins
with rare mintmarks in the other.

Next Spring

When I hear robins singing
that all relinquished things shall come again
and when bright April's golden promise comes to bloom,
then shall I put aside my heart's accustomed yearning
to know that soon my lover will be homeward turning.
My heart shall bid farewell the ache of winter's gloom
and say goodbye to cloudy skies and rain
when I hear robins singing.

Without

If I were blind and could not watch the late sun
melting into a simmering sea
or wish on the first starlight-starbright hope of evening,

it would not be the lost sunset
that would deprive me
but the oak-gold contour of your smile.

And your hand never rising in a benediction of heights
to which my earth-bound soul can never soar
(not the absence of a planet's borrowed light)
would leave me poor indeed.

If I were deaf, there is not a noble symphony that I would miss
so much as the melody of my name as you pronounce it.
Your slightest anger would put to shame
the most thunderous quaking of the earth.

Speak then, and let the earth revolve.
Smile, and let the oceans undulate.
If you did not sound or shine for me,
I could not be.

Wedding Song

I cannot swear with any certainty
that I will always feel as I do now,
loving you with the same fierce ecstasy,
needing the same your lips upon my brow,
nor can I promise stars forever bright
or vow green leaves will never turn to gold.
I cannot see beyond this present night
to say what promises the day may hold.
And yet, I know my heart must follow you
high up to hilltops, low through vales of tears,
through golden days and days of somber hue,
and love will only deepen with the years,
becoming sun and shadow, wind and rain,
wine that grows mellow, bread that will sustain.

Arrival

Let me come into your days
easily
not as a strange knock at the door
of a busy housewife
or a bell's intrusion upon sleep.
Let me
just be there
like a pillow on the sofa,
familiar and expected.

Let me be
something that always was
and needs to be:
reassuring
and necessary
as sails and stars
and harbors that are home.

For You

How like a jasmine you bloom
in my garden of remembrance!

Daily you bless me with the fragrance
of once-love.

Even in winter, April small buds promise
the casual touch of hands.

Perhaps I will dream you tonight.
It is there you will love me forever

as perennial blossoms burgeon
in ever-renewing spring.

Deep

Toward the deep clear waters that you are
my dry roots yearn

To stir and probe past clay and sand to wells of being
is all my hope

To watch one withering leaf grow green
and turn to kiss the sun

Small Wind

Let my being whistle down the corridor of your memory
like a small wind under a door it cannot enter.
Though you may never know that you are listening,
you may still turn your ear a moment sometimes
to catch the love I always will be singing
and understand the music,
however lost the words may be.

Signature

Messages sing toward you along taut wires,
sizzling across electric feathers of snow.

Without warning, bulbs burst into brightness
all along the highway; sometimes
fire engines clang with metal urgency.

Do little bells tingle you silverly awake
some mornings? Do flints of sunlight
strike against your skin, ignite?
And do you rise then with inexplicable
joy and energy?

I send you messages along taut wires,
singing, incendiary. Are you
receiving them? Do you
recognize their signature?

Old Shoe

I'm an old shoe.
I'm made of good leather;
I wear well.

When the new shoe pinches
I'll be here, carelessly
tossed under the bed but waiting
and ready to give relief.

If I had nothing to clothe
I'd lose my shape and go flat.
So put me on. Wear me
in comfort and with ease.

Old Wine

When your spring-vital rains refreshed
my own parched season,
I tasted joy sufficient for my life-old thirst,
sufficient in abundance to be stored in casks
safe from time and tears.

Now in the year of drought in my heart's country,
I sip remembered tang of wine and dew
(full measure of your kisses' goodness)
and find somehow each cask
replenished with the taking.

Song for a Season

Through winter's chill, stay warm.
Through blast of wind, keep steady and secure.
December holds no threat this year, no harm
to one protected lovingly. Endure

as seeds endure beneath earth's vigilance.
Some little wisp of dream is all we know
perhaps of sun and green and sustenance
amid the frost and snow.

But this sufficiency
I offer you for balm: that love and dreams
are life's most tangible reality.
It's time alone that *seems*.

Anniversary Song

How good it is to let our memory wander
and travel back across the fruitful years
to count how many miles we've walked together!
On pinnacles of dreams, through vales of tears,
along the level ground of every day
we've made our way.

In sickness and in health, in joy and sadness,
together, side by side, sunshine and shade,
we've worked toward common goals, found satisfaction
in all the hours of which our years are made.
All things were possible because we shared,
because we cared.

And after all these years, we still hold dearest
of all life's blessings anywhere on earth
the trust and honor that we give each other,
the love that gave our other blessings birth.
Praise be that I am yours by plan divine,
that you are mine!

TRINITY:
A DREAM
SEQUENCE

Trinity: A Dream Sequence

1.

I will sing you songs until your heart can hear
their silences,
shine my lamp until your eyes perceive
the dark from which it springs.

Through the entangled forest of my dreams
your dream will falter toward me,
and some day we shall meet.

2.

I know you have to find me in your dreaming.
You could not enter mine with so much ease
if the paths were unfamiliar to your feet.

You have to wake and find me lingering,
some wisp of misty memory
not completely lost.

If not, why do you come uncalled into my sleep,
your voice quieting howling winds,
your fingers' touch lighting up stars?

So must the fog lift over waking valleys
until one day in consciousness you call my name.

3.

Already I have forgotten the phrase
that rocketed to mind. It escapes me
like a dream untold until too late.

Now I labor over words, trying to capture
mountains of somewhere: towering out of mist and haze,
power and height and granite roadways to infinity.

I would give you the song if I could remember,
if I could only recall what star exploded in my dream.

4.

You would not recognize yourself if I should tell you
what truth emerges from your levity and mirth.
Your depth is so disguised that even you
would be surprised to see your image in the glass
I hold. But let it be.
Enough that I discover you
over and over, dream and dream again,
in each encounter, and I have a secret
I cannot tell you.

5. (Morning Song)

I give you love and joy and all good things
that summer brings:
leaf in a sympathetic breeze, a dawn
to wish upon,

cool grasses' dew, benevolence of rain,
release from pain,
burst of a blossom, sustenance of prayer,
the sun's first flare.

First breath of dawn, the sky's first blue I bring,
a song to sing,
and peace beside a slow and sinuous stream
where you can dream.

My days' first thought, my nights' last consciousness,
my dreamed caress,
rebirth of joy and love each day anew.
These are for you.

6.

You walk a highway where pale lilies blow
in the white glare of noon

breathing cold purity
in approved scentlessness.

Come to the garden: I am not ashamed
to call you.

Shadows of Eden beckon you to musk
of warm, forbidden roses,
dark scarlet petals of discovery.

Come and unmask the secret face of night.
In fragrant fields find truth so bold
and so magnificent that jealous gods
would name it sacrilege to walk therein.

7. Commandment

The tablet shattered when you touched my hand.
God may have winced
but I am not convinced
He did. No vision of a Promised Land

ever evoked such joy. If law opposes
a sin so fair,
then I will gladly bear
the ancient punishment that humbled Moses.

8.

I will be your Eve,
fulfill your need of conscience for a name
and thereby give you peace.

Brand this I give you Apple of Destruction,
Lure of the Golden Death;
it may be so.

But oh, before we trail the long descent,
driven from paradise into despair,
reach out and share my joy.

It well may be
the flame we stretch our longing toward
is not perdition only but a star.

9.

Was it really you all the time,
you who first stumbled upon me
behind some sea-soaked rock?
Or was it I who, first surprised to see you there,
came running then through the salt wind,
feet wet, hair flying?

Who opened the door?
Who entered first and which one followed?
Out of breath, out of mind, I woke
in the house somebody built of crusted sand.
(To trap us or to give us peace, or both?)
I never knew but thought I knew *I* built it
and led you there.
Was it you?

10.

I will not betray you; do not be afraid
my eyes will tell the secret never told
by word or touch—that you have come to me
in Time, walked me through rich meadows,
made revelations on hilltops in the sunlate afternoon
till shadows fell to cover us in Eden.

Now I will pass through millenniums of silence
before I tell philosopher or sage
who stands upright in the center of the universe.

11.

Thine is the kingdom of the fervent stars
and gilded dreams
of silver-singing night.

Thine is the power of the surging wind
to clear the web
of darkness from my birth.

Thine is the glory of the limitless,
the far-borne hope
of all my upward flight.

Forever be thy face my loveliness,
thy hands the wings
that lift me from the earth.

12. Trinity

Of the Father and the father and the Son
you are most glorious and noble
and most needful (lover, too, made one).

Of the water and the fire and the blood
most cleansed and sacrificial,
baptized and drowned and still borne breathing
by the flood.

Of the wine and the plea and the prayer
and the hill hard traveled, climbed in pain,
and the garden known alone in despair;

trinity in burden, acquiescence, suffering,
flame and lily and denial of the will,
joy and sadness and the hopelessness to sing;

of the spirit and the flower and the dew
you are most You.

13.

I kissed your feet,
poured fragrant oil upon their weariness
and dried them with my hair.

You did not care
that I had sinned but blessed me

and you were blessed in turn,
raised to most high potential
by my adoration.

14.

Mine were the arms shielding your infancy.
I dipped you in the Styx, yet left you vulnerable,
cradled your weakness, sought to ease your sighs
to no avail.

I was Jocasta, too,
played to an unsuspecting Oedipus.

I was the woman you gave up to John.
I watched you crucified,
saw your head drop in final-seeming death
and wept.

15.

If you should die
I would resurrect you
from stone-locked sepulcher.
From your discarded raiment
I would raise such triumph to the sky
of truth and wonder
as would rock some universe
unknown to this.

16.

All love is God, all love
is everything, eternal drama all-
encompassing.

17.

I tottered on the rim of consciousness
watching with fretful eyes the hours stage
their jumbled drama. I sobbed out
your name and waited for your voice
to drown me in its tenderness.

What dream did you nestle in?
What peace pillowed your head
and muffled the sound of my calling?

A bell's insistence jangled the day awake,
but I am still afraid.

18.

Stark day corrodes the silver of the dream a little, yes.
And caution insulates gloved fingers now
against enchantment of a certain touch.
But the splendor does not vanish
because you avert your eyes
nor the music cease to shiver
because your words are quick and cold.

I had to tell you.
Turn away if you must; I always knew
that you would have to turn away.

Still I can sing you songs
in silence more eloquent
than hope or triumph.

19.

These days I gave to you,
these heights I soared:

wept but was brave for you—
suffered, adored—
made and created you

out of my need;
love that awaited you
nurtured the seed.

Wonder of miracle
circled your face,
magical, lyrical
creature of grace.
Time stopped and stayed for you.
Reverent, proud
infidels prayed for you,
saw you and bowed:

Glorious trinity
fashioned of air!

So much divinity
man could not bear,
so it is earth for you,
temporal god,
mortal rebirth for you
straight from the sod.

I shall not weep for you,
sorrow or smile,
reach out in sleep for you
(after a while).

What sins they say of us
ours be the cost.
Then let them pray for us,
pardoned, but lost.

20.
What if you saw me lying there
like stone? What if you had to see?
What if you had to know and share?

What if you had to say the words
to bless or curse me (knowing you
were curse and blessing)? What if swords

of dream and passion smote you still
while I, removed from wanting, lay
redeemed from thunder, fire and will?

What things life does not grant to see
you'd know as I'd know, being dead.
What I had been, then you would be.

Suppose you had to bid the year
be kind or cruel for my sake?
What if you had to know my fear

and still you had to bless the wine
and break the bread from that day on
and kiss the cup that wasn't mine?

You could not face the tortured days;
you could not lift a crucifix,
impart the benediction's grace.

So I must live, and so release
your nights from penitence and pain
and give you peace—and give you peace.

STORMY
WEATHER

Misconception

I shall remember how we met and parted
upon a hill at dusk of every day
to greet the first star in its shy appearance
and bid farewell the flaming sun's last ray.

Oh, when we met, Apollo in his glory
cast all his radiant beauty on your hair,
and twilight's gleaming roseate hues were mingled
with morning stars that were still lingering there.

What witchery the purple shadow uses
on darkening hillsides in the setting sun!
I used to think your eyes were truly lighted
with precious gems and pure gold finely spun.

Now that I see you, not in flame and sunshine
but by the frigid bleakness of the sea,
my sad heart whispers just how dull and tarnished
and stripped of gold you have turned out to be.

Where Do We Go?

Where do we go, my love? Where do we go?
The silver of young trees to ash has blown;
the sun's bright gold is but a burned-out flame.
Where do we go, Love, after love has flown?

We sing but empty songs with weary voices;
with weary hearts we mourn for what has fled;
a little spark that kept our world from darkness.
Where do we go, Love, when that spark is dead?

Like driftwood drifting idly in a stream,
like silent ghosts in a bewildered dream,
like hearts that are not what they used to seem,
we wander, Love—where, after love has gone?

Where do we go, my love? Where do we go?
To bury love in cold, responseless sod
or do we weep to drown the love we feel,
or do we laugh? Or do we search for God?

Seasons Have to Pass

The frail warm dream lay shattered like a glass,
a thousand fragments crushed beneath your feet.
(Time is not stagnant: seasons have to pass.
Farewell, my dream, left wounded in the street.)

A cold wind blew like winter in July.
The doubtful ember sputtered in the rain.
(All lovely things must go; all dreams must die.
Not sighs or tears can bring them back again.)

Some dreams fade like the fragrance of a rose;
some fall and crash like fine and fragile glass,
but none can stay. The golden minute goes.
(Time is not stagnant; seasons have to pass.)

After Parting

Yes, I did suffer though the changing seasons
turned green to gold and gold to barren gray.
The moon did tarnish, and it had its reasons
and sullen dawn blurred into sunless day.

So well you knew me that you did not wonder
if parting would condemn me to the pit.
You knew your words would rock my earth like thunder;
you never had a minute's doubt of it.

You knew, and yet you let the darkness take me.
Firm in your knowledge, still you went away.
Without a backward glance you could forsake me;
without regret you tore the mirth from May.

Yet in my heart you have been pardoned fully
for I no longer question destiny.
I know you felt compelled to go as truly
as Christ did when He turned to Calvary.

Funereal

I have dug you a grave
and laid you away in a cedar box
amid a mountain of tissue paper
and blue ribbons
and the delicate scent of age-old dreams.
I have buried all that I could
but there is still left
a quick, sharp pain
like a grain of salt in a wound.

How Shall I Face the Dawn?

How shall I face the dawn whose restless sleep
is tempest-torn and weighed with loss and dread?
How can I see the sun except to weep
or speak, except to say that hope is dead?

I have no wish to see another day
paled by the dream whose truth our lives deny.
I have no will to walk this barren way
alone in darkness, living but to die.

The fates have spoken doom upon my poor
frail dream, and darkness clouds the light.
I ask to feel the warmth and glow no more.
Let the March storm snuff out my flame tonight.

Two

How little I know you
can hardly hide behind your enigmatic smile.
How deeply shallow is your love I can only guess.

I will never tell you words that mean;
that would be suicide.
Only this much (and little) I am certain of.

In separate spheres we move
(circumferences touching randomly),
blest and tormented by our isolation,

always on the road to Delphi,
never getting there
but never turning back.

If we should ever arrive,
what good would it do to decipher the riddle
only to destroy the quest?

Congenital

I know what it means to give birth to a child already dying,
to watch unfocused eyes already shadowed over
with sickly glaze of doom.

Death is in your touch.
Even as we kiss, your snake-cold mouth
condemns me to the tomb.

Love was aborted
long before you called my name,
and I am helpless to undo the business of the womb.

If Not in Summer

If not in summer, then not at all will you come,
and I had better dig my yearning into doom
than wish a corpse to breath and blood again.

If not in starlight, then not at all will you hold me,
and nights more luminous than this will tarnish
before you say my name.

Not candlelight will call you?
Not dawn—not even spring?
Well then, not anything.

If There Were Songs to Sing

If there were songs to sing I would have sung them
in spring, at dawn, wherever willows bent their way
into a stream.

If there were stars to catch I would have wrung them
from startled velvet midnights, blazed them into day
out of a dream.

You of all people surely ought to know
(if anyone should be so wise)
how love inhibited, not set me free,
and lured me down a road I did not choose to go,
diverting me from paradise
toward shadows of Gethsemane.

Discards

I emptied your wastebasket the other day
and found the star I gave you once
when we went walking on air.

There was a seashell too.
I remember the morning I scraped
the crust of sand away
and handed you its pearl-dawn iridescence
to keep.

I started to save them for you
thinking you might some day regret
your haste in throwing them away.

But when I saw the gaudy bauble
that had replaced my honest song
perched brazenly on your desk, I realized

that what the giver offers
gets altered sometimes in the passing
from heart to hand.

I tossed the shell and star
into my own wastebasket this afternoon.
The song will have to wait
until another day.

Afterthought

I would like to believe we loved each other once—
that you were my Undiscovered Room
in a house full of mirrors and windows
and I, your paper Popperjack
snapped into small explosions from the folded air
to soar you into supersonic flight.

But the winds of many voices
have stretched you open to such constant height
that no rare single breath can lift you anymore

and to tell the truth
my house has narrowed to such stifling darkness
that I no longer seek the hidden room,
only a door that opens outward
into a limitless expanse of light.

Post-Script

Still let me find your guarded eyes
as deep with longing as before,
your hand as warm, though lips and thighs
    consent no more.

Though passion was our only prize,
our only region to explore,
what pain it is to realize you
    meant no more.

Repeat again those easy lies
of dreams that night seemed fated for,
then leave me to my secret sighs
    content no more.

Star Journey

Alone I tiptoe through the stars
precipitously steep,
watchful lest I wake the gods
and angels from their sleep.

Alone I climb the secret hills
unknown to mortal feet
and stand upon a peak where you
and I can never meet.

To you who do not dream, I am
a gently tilted head,
a voice that chatters, earth aware,
a gay mouth painted red.

Better that you possess a cold
impenetrable stone
than woo my body while my soul
tips through the stars alone.

The Divorcee

This house was gay once, once upon a time.
Its lamps burned bright and laughter shook its walls.
Its doors swung wide, and many feet would climb
its stairs to enter into welcome halls.

But there were, too, anxieties and fears
and sleepless nights that held no hope for day.
The laughter was too mingled with the tears
and I was wise to go another way.

Now I am lonely and the house is still
and no one comes into this darkened room
or sees the dust upon the windowsill,
and no one cares, and no one shares my gloom.

And here in bitter thought I sit and weep,
remembering when a baby used to cry,
and here I pass my nights and cannot sleep
and curse the dawn and wish that I could die.

Souvenir

This is not what I meant to keep
I thought of bitter-bright rememberings
pressed petals of forget-me-nots
or once-bold daffodils

not
this hardness
not
these brittle stalks of
weeds

If Love Were All

Stars have their price; with silver they are bought.
If love were all, to worship at their shrine
would be enough. But darling, I have sought
their radiant brilliance and they are not mine.

Paupers and beggars, we, amid the gleaming
so distant that our hands can only reach.
In darkness we have lost ourselves in dreaming,
knowing the tragedy that dreams would teach.

But oh, what light, what rays of sudden splendor
to eager fingers through the night would fall,
soothing the bruise that unkind gods left tender,
if the young, faithful heart in love were all!

Haiku #2

Rain slashes dark like
a switchblade. You are the rain.
I am bleeding night.

Again

When I do come, perhaps you will not recognize me.
Time will have had her way with you and, tired and old,
you may not care that once I was the dream you cherished
in times when harsh reality was much less bold.

You may forget that summer once was fair and fragile,
fairer than any other June will ever say,
and pass me by on some strange street and never utter
the words you said would live again some better day.

The Prisoners

What loves I hold who never recognize
their own captivity!
I keep them prisoners within such secret cells
they never guess they are not free.
Time rubs their tarnished metal bright,
restores fragmented honor whole—
adorns their nakedness with lustrous cloth
I weave, dispense, control.

They do not know I own them now,
that they are mine to keep
in small, barred corners of remembering,
secure and deep.

Somewhere in the City

You are somewhere in the city, lost to me
but sharing buildings, skyline, traffic signals,
street names, rush hours, and street scenes,
sharing unconsciously things we do not share
by purpose anymore.
And though we do not meet, and though our feet
do not strike the same pavement at the same time,
you are mine as the city is mine.
You and the city are one.
The city cannot enclose me in its foggy arms
without your arms, too, holding me in a loose embrace.

Somewhere in the city you are driving someone somewhere
or telephoning or taking a bath
or making love or watching a movie or working
or polishing the metal on the car you are so proud of
or getting sleepy over wine
or telling jokes or playing a jukebox in a bar.

How many times have I barely missed you
by one block or one door or a one-way street?

Somewhere you are forgetting me
and making of me nothing—
no more than the song you listen to
or the joke you tell.

My eyes will be impassable as fog
if we should ever meet again,
as bright as streetlights,
as shallow as rain, as hard as steel.
The soft soul-eyes you knew will be for you
the barren city,
the city without love or hope or mercy or desire,
without remembrance, without nostalgia,

without soul.
And you will not realize or understand
how often I caress you
when the downtown lights blink on
and the traffic signals change from red to green.

Time Is No Thief

Only the minutes, not the years, are ours
and yet, Time is no thief.
Our love is not a time-encumbered thing.
Minutes will go
like raindrops leaking through reluctant roofs,
but what is lost?

Oh, say not, *I have loved a little while,*
a brief, uncertain day ruled by the clock,
then she was gone. Say not this empty thing.
Though I shall go and all the years remaining
will brood that other lips, not ever ours again,
        must meet,
oh, do not sigh, my love, and do not be afraid.

Earth is not ours, but we have touched and held the stars.
The perfect golden minutes slip away
and yet,
Time is no thief.

Always

If one autumn you should see,
    out of season,
robins in a leafless tree
    without reason,
blue amid a somber sky,
    stars in daytime,
never doubt that it is I
    bringing Maytime.

Never think I will not stay
    always near you.
Sorrow need not come your way;
    doubt will fear you.
If this love you cherished so
    seems denied you,
know that where your footsteps go,
    I'm beside you.

Nocturne II: Still

Midnight streetlights beckon me
to a certain house on a certain nameless street.
The windows are darkly shuttered.
Somewhere beyond them (having yawned
through newsmen's dooms an hour ago) you sleep.
I ease my car into the blueblack peace,
the fretful motor purring, purring now.

Were you to stir and glance into the throbbing night,
you would see only a long still shadow
across an ordinary street.
You would not sense the heavy-blossomed fuschia branches—
you would forget that it is April once again.

Blow out the candle as you will.
The farthest star still watches, the loneliest shadow
leans toward you still.

Severance

If you have forgotten, then I say
I have forgotten, too.
I give you back your soul
and send you gladly on your way.

Whenever a new moon rises,
an old sun sets. I know that,
and I know I have to let you go.

But when dreams, wild as prairie broncos,
burst from their bonds
and gallop toward each other
defying choice and wisdom,
sleep has no tether that can keep them apart.

Without Condition

All these years
I have loved you
without condition of return,

laid my sacrifices
at the altar of your need.
Spring

never spiraled through
reluctant soil without
my touch, or
summer

surged through sun
and azure wind
without my presence
at your rebirth.

I have wished you
cardinals and lemonade,
lake water stroking your hand,
sunrise

and songs
my frail voice could not
sing but only
say.

When the first
green leaf turned
to scarlet or gold,
I have been

there always.
When winter blanketed

dead leaves in snow, I have
been there.

So what if now
another voice sustains you,
another hand teaches you what
love means?

It's all right, it really is
all right because

I have loved you all
these years
without
condition of return.

Packrat

My trouble is
I always try to save
everything

old clocks and calendars
expired words buried
in open graves

But hoarded grains of sand
keep shifting as rivers
redefine boundaries and seasons

Lengths of old string
rolled into neat balls
neither measure nor bind

nor do shelves laden with rancid sweets
preserve
what ants continually nibble away

Love should be eaten
while it is ripe
and then the pits discarded

Lord give me at last
one cracked bowl holding
absolutely nothing

Never Without Remembrance

Never without remembrance will we meet,
never our fingers touch in simplest greeting
without a kiss implied, the other's name
pronounced or heard, however fleetingly,
without that word rekindling into flame
a possibility that flares, then dies
as guilt and caution warn us what is wise.

Let it be sufficient that our hands' caress
stirs embers still
when all our dreams are ashes.

Impressions

1.

And the blue dusk folded us into a narrow room
and the snow draped its silence across our window.
Behind our temporary door we sank into layers of
peace.

2.

We blew up promises like bright balloons
and sent them sailing on the festive air—
with strings attached.

3.

Suddenly unsheathed, the blade of morning
slashed our warm pulsating darkness
into ribbons of pain.

No Choice

All that I want of you I take.
It's not your privilege to offer or withhold.

The sun climbs the morning and has no say
in who receives its benediction.

Rain falls and can't select
who is to be refreshed.

You are. I take from you
all that I need.

The Time Is Now

What difference does it make now that the snows are falling?
These bare dark trees have no remembrances of spring.
No flowers are blooming now; there are no bright birds calling
and winter casts its spell of death on everything.

Why mourn the loss of azure Junes? Who would remember
in these bleak days how bright with hope the skies could be?
What good are golden summer dreams in mid-December?
What pleasure now holds dawn's fantastic ecstasy?

Alas, the magic hour is past for love and roses.
They did not come, they will not come, but should I weep?
The time has come to turn from every door that closes,
to turn from dreams and settle down to peaceful sleep.

Now is no time for grieving over last year's splendor.
It is of no more consequence than last year's rain.
However sweet, however beautiful and tender,
it could not last; it will not ever live again.

O perished heart, your grief will pass just with the knowing
that yesterday has vanished and the time is now.
Who wants to keep the embers of a dead love glowing?
Who wants to sing and sigh forever anyhow?

Clock

I have lost track of time. The monster face
no longer rules me with its dozen eyes.
Freed from the boundaries of time and place

I do not need your kisses or your sighs.
On seas of space I drift without a shore,
the wisdom of the stars sufficient prize.

Praise be for strength and credence to restore
from iron hands of time's compulsive will
white winds and free directions to explore.

So shall my days be numberless until
the pain of you exists for me no more.

ABOUT THE AUTHOR

Naomi Long Madgett, poet laureate of Detroit since 2001, is author of ten books of poetry, most recently *Connected Islands*. She has edited two anthologies, including *Adam of Ife: Black Women in Praise of Black Men,* and is author of a textbook, *A Student's Guide to Creative Writing,* as well as her autobiography, *Pilgrim Journey.* Madgett is professor emerita of English at Eastern Michigan University.